Protect the Oceans
Act Locally

Written by Kerrie Shanahan

Flying Start
to Literacy®

T0363957

Contents

Introduction

Did you know that if you drop a piece of rubbish in a street it could end up in the ocean? How does this happen?

Rubbish dropped in the street is often washed along gutters and into stormwater drains. These drains empty into rivers or the sea. The rubbish pollutes the oceans.

Many people around the world are working to stop this from happening.

Rubbish
in street

Rubbish gets
washed into drains

Drains empty into rivers, lakes and seas

Rubbish pollutes the ocean

Chapter 1

The rubbish problem

Ocean garbage patches

When rubbish ends up in the ocean, it gets moved around by winds and currents. Huge amounts of rubbish end up in the same place in the middle of the ocean. It becomes a garbage patch.

Over time, more and more rubbish is carried to the same part of the ocean and the garbage patch gets bigger and bigger. This trapped rubbish makes the water cloudy and polluted, and is dangerous for sea animals. Today there are several garbage patches in the oceans.

The Great Pacific Garbage Patch

One of the biggest garbage patches in the ocean is called the Great Pacific Garbage Patch. This garbage patch has millions of tiny pieces of plastic as well as some larger pieces of rubbish floating in it.

Scientists can't say exactly how big it is, but they think it is even bigger than the state of New South Wales in Australia.

Today, there are several garbage patches in the world's oceans.

garbage patch

Great Pacific Garbage Patch

It would be difficult and very costly to clean up all of the garbage patches in the ocean, but we can help to stop them growing.

Animals at risk

Oceans are home to many amazing animals, but the rubbish in the oceans is putting their lives at risk.

Sometimes, animals try to eat this rubbish or they get trapped in it. This can injure or kill the animals.

Every year about 100,000 sea animals such as whales, seals and sea turtles die because they try to eat plastic or they get tangled in it.

About one million sea birds also die each year by choking on plastic or becoming caught in it.

Chapter 2

Taking action

What can we do about rubbish in the oceans?

We cannot get rid of the rubbish that is already in the oceans, but there are things that we can do. If we look after our local environment, we are helping to stop rubbish ending up in the ocean. This will help to keep our oceans clean and the animals that live there safe.

All over the world there are people who believe they can make a difference. These people work together to clean up the places where they live.

Cleaning up the beach

Fiji

I'm Ata. I live near the beach on an island
in Fiji in the Pacific Ocean.

The people in my town know how important
it is to keep the ocean clean. We eat mainly
fish. We know that rubbish in the ocean
can harm fish and other sea animals.

The people in my town organise days where we come together to pick up rubbish. We pick up rubbish in our town and on the beach. This makes our town look cleaner and it also stops the rubbish being swept out to sea, polluting the ocean and injuring the animals.

Picking up rubbish in the lake

I'm Josh.   I live in the USA.

The lake near my home is very important
to our town.   People like to fish in the
lake, and they also like to swim and sail.
Over the years, the lake became polluted.
The fish were not good to eat.   It was not
a safe place to swim.

The people in my town decided to take action.
We picked up rubbish from around the lake.
We now do this several times a year and
each time we pick up many bags of rubbish.

The lake near my home runs into the ocean,
and so does any rubbish that is in or near
the lake. By picking up this rubbish, I am
helping to keep the ocean clean.

Cleaning up in the city

Australia

I'm Brody and I live in Sydney, Australia. Sydney is famous for its beautiful beaches. When it rains, the rainwater flows into drains, which run all the way to the ocean. As the water runs along, it picks up rubbish and sometimes this rubbish ends up on the beaches and in the ocean.

My family and I sometimes join with other people to help make our city look better. We clean up rubbish so that it does not litter the beaches and pollute the ocean. We also remove graffiti and grow new plants to create a healthy and beautiful environment.

Reducing plastics

Canada

I'm Karen. I live in Canada.

In my town, everyone is encouraged to recycle their plastic bags. Plastic bags often end up in street drains, rivers and eventually in the ocean. By recycling these bags, there is less chance that the bags end up in the ocean.

At my school we set up a plastic bag recycling bin. Now many school families bring their plastic bags to school where they are collected to be recycled.

We are helping to keep plastic bags off the streets and out of the oceans.

Chapter 3

What can you do?

All of these children believe that they can make a difference. You can help to improve the world too.

The first thing you can do is to make sure your rubbish goes where it should. By doing this, it will not end up in the ocean. You will be helping to protect our oceans and the animals that live there.

A note from the author

Although we are all helping to keep the world clean, we can't stop now. In my research, I was horrified to learn that there is still a massive amount of rubbish in the oceans. One particular mass of rubbish is called "The Great Pacific Garbage Patch". I can't believe how big this garbage patch is.

I hope we all continue to work together to help keep this amazing planet clean.